Shoot for the Moon

Other titles in the Hodder African Readers series

The Fearless Four	978 0340 940426
The Fearless Four: Hijack!	978 0340 940419
The Fearless Four and the Graveyard Ghost	978 0340 940358
The Fearless Four and the Smugglers	978 0340 940334
Dead Men's Bones	978 0340 940365
Twin Trouble	978 0340 940310
Sauna and the Drug Pedlars	978 0340 940402
The Power of Corruption	978 0340 940341
Magic, Mystery and Mister Prince	978 0340 940389
Time Bomb	978 0340 940327
God's Case: No Appeal	978 0340 940372
One Man, Two Votes	978 0340 940396
Dear Miss Winfrey	978 0340 984178
Madulo & Co.	978 0340 984185
The Button Bottle	978 0340 984222
The Mystery of Rukodzi Mountain	978 0340 984239
A Few Little Lies	978 0340 984154
Conquest & Conviviality	978 0340 984161
Secret Celebrity	978 0340 984208
No More Secrets	978 0340 984192

Shoot for the Moon

By Bridget Krone

Illustrated by Lois Neethling

AN HACHETTE UK COMPANY

Orders: please contact Hachette UK Distribution, Hely Hutchinson Centre, Milton Road, Didcot, Oxfordshire, OX11 7HH. Telephone: +44 (0)1235 827827. Email: education@hachette.co.uk. Lines are open from 9 a.m. to 5 p.m., Monday to Friday. You can also order through our website: www.hoddereducation.com

© Bridget Krone 2008
First published in this edition in 2008 by Hodder Education,
An Hachette UK Company
Carmelite House
50 Victoria Embankment
London EC4Y 0DZ

The authorised representative in the EEA is Hachette Ireland, 8 Castlecourt Centre, Dublin 15, D15 XTP3, Ireland (email: info@hbgi.ie)

Impression number   10 9 8 7
Year   2025

All rights reserved. Apart from any use permitted under UK copyright law, no part of this publication may be reproduced or transmitted in any form or by any means, electronic or mechanical, including photocopying and recording, or held within any information storage and retrieval system, without permission in writing from the publisher or under licence from the Copyright Licensing Agency Limited. Further details of such licences (for reprographic reproduction) may be obtained from the Copyright Licensing Agency Limited, www.cla.co.uk

Cover and illustration by Lois Neethlng
Typeset in 14/18 Bembo by Manoj Sookai
Printed by Clays Ltd
A catalogue record for this title is available from the British Library

ISBN: 978 0340 98 421 5

Shoot for the moon. Even if you miss it you will land among the stars.
– Les Brown

Chapter One

'Boipelo!'
'Boipelo!'
'Boi!'

I heard my grandmother calling me from her chair in the yard but I pretended not to hear because I was busy trying to get my friend Paki's cellphone to work. He'd got it cheaply from his cousin who had dropped it in a ditch. He said that we simply needed to dry the battery. Of course Paki didn't have any money for airtime, but it would look cool just carrying it around. I had opened the back of the phone and lots of tiny pieces lay on the bed. I didn't have any idea what I was doing.

'Boipelo!'

I looked up to see my grandmother hobbling into the house.

'I knew you were here, you lazy child. I'm watching the washing dry and I need you to come and read to me.'

My grandmother has very bad eyesight. She wears glasses as thick as the bottom of a Coke bottle. My father says that is why she is so grumpy sometimes.

'Auntie Shirley got me a whole pile of magazines. You can read me those.' She hobbled back outside and sat back heavily into her chair.

I didn't want to read to her. I knew those magazines: they were full of old TV schedules and horoscopes. And I wanted to get this cellphone back together before Paki came round. He would be here soon. So I fiddled a bit longer.

'Boipelo!' shouted my grandmother sounding angry.

I shot off the bed and grabbed the first magazine from where it had been stuffed under the bed. I skidded to a stop in the dust under the peach tree. 'OK,' I said. 'What shall I read?'

My grandmother leaned over my shoulder and pointed with one knobbly finger to an article on the cover of the magazine. I don't think she could even read what it said.

'Right.' I turned to page 85 and began reading about 'Twenty-five Festive Ideas for Mince'. I read for about ten minutes. Then I yawned and shifted in the dust. My grandmother had fallen asleep.

I flipped the pages lazily and read my horoscope which was about two years out of date:

While the moon is in the phase of Sagittarius you can expect major changes for the better in your life. Your love life will show a marked improvement as many people will be attracted by your zest for life. Your lucky number is 25.

'Who writes this stuff?' I wondered. I tried to think back to the date of the magazine – two years ago. Had I experienced any 'major changes'? There had been no major changes in my life since my mother had died when I was a baby. My father had lost his job when the cheese factory closed. That was a major change but it had happened about eleven years ago. We have been living in the concrete block house number 437 for the past eight years. Every day I go to school. I hang out with Paki and some other friends around the café or the soccer field. Sometimes we fish for

carp in the river. Once I went to Kokstad to go to the doctor for a bad case of worms. I think I would have noticed if I'd experienced any 'major changes for the better'.

'Nothing *ever* changes here,' I thought as I flipped through the rest of the magazine.

Chapter Two

My eye was caught by one particular story: 'Man Trades Paper Clip for a House'.

I remember thinking that was impossible. Who would want to swap a paper clip for a house? It was a big house too – there was a photo – a double-storey, wooden house in a town called Kipling in Canada. There was also a photo of Kyle MacDonald, the man who had traded the paper clip and ended up with the house. He was smiling. I rolled over onto my stomach and started to read:

A year ago, on the 12th of July 2005, Montreal resident Kyle MacDonald advertised a red paper clip on the Internet. His plan was to keep trading, each time with something of a higher value – until he reached his goal: a house.

'I couldn't afford the down payment on a house,' said Kyle MacDonald. 'I was feeling

depressed and was staring at this red paper clip on my desk when I got my idea. I decided to advertise it on the Internet and see if anyone would give me something in exchange for it. I was happy to trade for anything as long as it was of a higher value.'

Well it took him a year, 14 trades and many trips all over Canada and the USA but his dream of owning a house has come true. Exactly a year after he first advertised the paper clip, on the 12th of July 2006, the town of Kipling handed MacDonald the keys to his house.

'My first trade was for a pen that was shaped like a fish. I traded that for a ceramic door handle. Someone in Massachusetts had read my website and offered to trade me a Coleman stove in exchange for the door handle ... I advertised the Coleman stove with the offer of a cooked meal and traded that for a small electric generator. Then someone in New York City offered to trade the generator for a keg of beer and a neon Budweiser sign.'

'By now a lot of people were reading my website and were getting excited by the direction

I was going in. A guy who was the host of a talk radio show in Montreal gave me a great break when he offered to trade a snow mobile for the keg of beer. He mentioned me on his radio station and that gave me a lot of publicity. Suddenly people wanted to interview me and I made guest appearances on Canadian and Japanese TV as well as "Good Morning America". On one of these appearances I mentioned as a joke that the only place I would not be prepared to travel to make a trade was a town called Yahk in British Columbia. Well you can guess what happened. The good citizens of Yahk decided to make an offer on the snow mobile and in exchange they offered a trip to Yahk including airfares, meals and skiing. Someone offered me a supply truck in exchange for the trip. I was then offered a recording contract which I traded for a year's free rent in Phoenix, Arizona. I traded that for an afternoon with superstar Alice Cooper. At this point I made a risky exchange and traded the Alice Cooper experience for a rare snow globe – you know, one of those plastic ornaments that encloses a little scene. When you shake it, it churns up a little snow storm. A famous actor in America, Corbin Bernsen, is a collector of these snow globes and he offered me a role in his next movie in exchange for this one. Where I live, a part in a movie is serious currency. This is where the town of Kipling came in on the deal. By now I had generated a lot of publicity for my quest and the people of Kipling figured that it would help to put their town on the map and attract tourists if they were able to offer me a house in their town. They decided to hold a talent contest in the town for the movie role.'

'And that is the story of how I traded a red paper clip for a house!'

Paki had arrived to collect his cellphone. He had wandered into the house and came out with his eyebrows raised, holding a fistful of tiny pieces.

'Don't worry about the cellphone,' I said. 'I've got an idea and I want you to listen.' I read him the story out loud.

Chapter Three

Paki looked at me and shook his head.

'So? What's your big idea?'

'I'm going to do the same thing as this Kyle MacDonald guy. I'm going to trade stuff . . . and try to get a new house.'

'How are you going to do that?' He looked at me as if I were crazy. 'You don't have the Internet. You'll have to break into the school strong-room to even *look* at a computer. How are you going to travel around the country making these trades? Do you think Mr Qokela is going to give you lifts in his taxi? You've forgotten man, you live in Cedarville. These kinds of things only happen to people who live in . . .' he grabbed the magazine from me and scanned the story, 'in . . . Montreal.'

'I don't know,' I replied. 'I'll work something out. The first thing I have to do is find something to trade.'

I went inside to look for something. It took a while for my eyes to adjust to the dark after being in the sunlight outside.

Paki followed me and started pulling things out and making silly suggestions.

'Hey! Boi! What about this tin cup? No, no wait! Ladies and gentlemen! Who will give me a large house in exchange for this . . . BUCKET?'

I looked around our house with new eyes. I knew every bump of its grey concrete walls, every wooden beam in the tin roof. The linoleum floor curled like old bread in the corners and the walls were blackened in places from candle smoke and the paraffin stove. We had two rooms: my father's bed and a wardrobe was on one side of the dividing wall and my grandmother's bed, the kitchen and the sink was on the other side. I slept on a foam mattress which was pushed under my grandmother's bed during the day.

I opened the wardrobe hoping for inspiration. But a pile of clothes and a stack of bright orange traffic cones fell out and hit me on the head. I wondered if I could trade a traffic cone but actually they belonged to my father. He had a job with the Municipal Road Maintenance project this month. They rotate the job so that different people get a chance to earn some money. Most people are unemployed in our town. At the end of the month someone else will take his job and he will be unemployed again.

Then I saw the clay cow. It was in the back corner of the cupboard. I'd made it at school about a year ago. Our teacher Mrs Mlando had sent us off to the river to get the clay and we'd had to make these dumb animals when we'd arrived back in class. Most of the boys had made oxen with big horns. But my horns had fallen off so many times I'd given up trying to attach them and turned the stupid thing into a cow.

'OK,' I said to Paki, 'I have found the first thing to trade. Now I will need your help to make a poster. Come on, you can draw.' I handed him a ballpoint pen and tore a piece of paper out of one of my large exercise books.

Paki sighed and rolled his eyes. But he took the piece of paper out of my hand, spread it out on the floor and began to draw.

Chapter Four

Paki drew a very good picture of the clay cow and wrote 'One clay cow' in big letters at the top of the poster. Under the picture he wrote 'TO TRADE for anything. Offers to be made to Boipelo Xaba.'

I grabbed the poster and the clay cow. We crept past my sleeping grandmother and ran up onto the road that led into the village. As we walked we had a good look at the houses to decide which would be a good one to live in. I could see Paki was starting to get a little bit more excited by my idea.

'What about that one?' He pointed to an old house with a tin roof and a wide veranda. There was a huge vegetable garden at the back which seemed to be full of overgrown onions and half-bricks.

'Not too bad,' I said, 'but it belongs to Mrs Jackson and she's been living there for about a hundred years. I'm looking for something a little more . . . modern.'

'OK,' said Paki, 'tell me about your dream house.'

'Well it must have electricity,' I started. 'And I must have my own bedroom. So at least three bedrooms. There will be a room for the TV and a kitchen with running water. We'll have a big lounge suite and one of those huge wall units.'

'For the hi-fi,' added Paki.

'And a proper stove for cooking.'

'And ceiling boards so you don't freeze in winter and boil in summer.'

'An inside toilet!'

'An outside room for me so I can come and stay.'

'Painted walls!'

'A garden?'

'Yes, but not too many flower beds and stuff. You want a nice big space where you can kick a soccer ball.'

By the time we reached the café, it was like I had already moved in to my imaginary house.

'OK, now we need to decide where to put up the poster,' I said as I came back down to earth.

'We need somewhere that is going to attract a lot of people.'

'Well I think that would have to be... Montreal,' joked Paki, 'because there's nowhere in this *nowhere town* of Cedarville that attracts a lot of people.'

'The library?'

'No ways. Only the old aunties go there. And a few school kids. I think we need a place where there is going to be some traffic. Kyle MacDonald had the whole of Canada and the USA reading his website.'

Well the obvious place was the café. It was not the World Wide Web but it was right opposite the garage. People coming to fill up with petrol often came across the road to buy a newspaper or a cooldrink at the café.

The plan was starting to take shape.

Chapter Five

First we needed to get permission from Mrs Viljoen, the café owner, to put up the poster on her wall.

'But what are you hoping to get for your clay cow?' she asked.

I could tell she didn't understand what my plan was about. And it did start to sound very silly when I told her about Kyle MacDonald and how he had traded his red paper clip for a house.

'Look,' said Mrs Viljoen, 'I'm very busy today. Dana didn't arrive for work and I have to do everything myself. You boys can put up your poster. But I don't want any nonsense. I've got no time for nonsense. Is that clear?' She looked at us sternly over her glasses and handed us a bit of Prestick to stick up our poster.

'OK Mrs Viljoen.'
'Thank you Mrs Viljoen.'
And we were out of the café in a flash.

We stuck up the poster on the wall that faced the road and waited for something to happen.

It didn't take long. There was a small crowd outside the bottle store next door, young guys who didn't have work. They seemed to spend most of their days hanging around there. Three of them walked slowly over and looked at the poster.

'A clay cow?' asked Luvo in a voice that made it sound like I was offering a dirty sock or a rotten potato.

They all turned to look at me as if I were mad in the head.

'Yes,' said Paki. 'He wants to swap it for anything that has a higher value. This guy in Canada did it with a red paper clip and he eventually got a house.'

They all hooted with laughter. 'Well I'll give you something that has a higher value,' said Luvo, and he picked up an empty, silver pie foil that was lying on the ground near the rubbish bin. He held it out with a look of mock seriousness.

The other two laughed and slapped the wall. Then they all did high fives with each other and walked back to the bottle store. We could see them entertaining the rest of the guys with the story as soon they were all pointing at us, laughing and enjoying the joke.

Paki clicked his tongue and stared straight ahead. I put the clay cow in the pocket of my shorts and held it tightly.

Then three of our friends arrived: Jude, Mawili and Prince. They had come to buy a loose cigarette. I don't know where they'd got the money. They all stared at the poster.

'So where's the clay cow?' asked Mawili.

I pulled it out of my pocket.

'And if we give you something you will give us *that*?' I could tell they didn't think it was such a great deal.

By now I was regretting this plan. It had sounded so simple at home but it seemed so stupid and complicated now that it was out in public.

But Jude seemed to think it might work. 'Come guys,' he said. 'Let's go and see what we can find.'

They all ran off down the street.

About five minutes later they were back. They'd brought a whole crowd of children with them. Some of the younger ones seemed to think I was handing out sweets or something and they stood in front of me holding out their hands.

Prince pushed them aside. 'Here,' he said. 'Is this the sort of thing you want?'

He held out an old shoe that he'd found down by the railway line.

'No, that's not what I had hoped for,' I said, irritated.

'What about this?' Someone pushed an old toy car with no wheels under my nose.

'If I give you this, will I get the house?' asked one moron who tried to offer me a library book.

Everyone was pushing and shoving and trying to get me to look at the rubbish they had brought. Some of them were even raiding the rubbish bin for stuff. They were all shouting and laughing.

Mrs Viljoen came out and shouted at us.

'Paki and Boipelo!' she yelled above the noise. 'I said I didn't want any nonsense. And this . . .' she waved her arm at the crowd of children, 'is

NONSENSE! Everybody must go home. Boi you can stay here by yourself.'

She disappeared inside the café.

Everyone went home and left me sitting outside the café under my stupid poster. Paki turned to wave at me but I pretended not to see him and stared down the road.

Chapter Six

There was a bit of traffic that morning; a few farmers came to get the *Kokstad Advertiser* and a litre of milk and some other people came to buy green soap and Boxer tobacco. Some of them read my poster and one woman patted my head as she walked past as if I were a baby or a pet dog. I suppose Mrs Viljoen must have told them what I was doing.

'This is just too embarrassing,' I thought, and turned round to take down the poster and go home.

Suddenly Mrs Viljoen stuck her head out of the café doorway.

'Come Boi. You might as well help me if you're going to sit there all day. I don't know what has happened to Dana.'

I followed her into the shop. She pointed to a pile of thick slices of white bread and some sliced polony.

'I need you to wrap two slices of bread and two slices of polony in this plastic.' She pointed to a roll of thin, sticky plastic.

I wrapped about ten packs very tightly using as little plastic as I could and then I swept the floor of the storeroom. When I was finished sweeping I wiped the big fridge and carefully replaced the three packets of Rama margarine and two pieces of fried chicken that took up a whole shelf.

'You can stock the fridge with these cooldrinks now,' said Mrs Viljoen from behind the till. She pointed to a pile of Cokes, Fantas and Cream Sodas stacked up against the wall.

I lined them up neatly in tidy rows on two shelves of the fridge, making sure they all faced the same direction. Then I swept the shop and picked up some rubbish that was lying outside on the pavement.

'Thank you Boi. You've done a good job,' said Mrs Viljoen as she peered over her glasses at me.

She paused and then she said, 'Now bring me that clay cow. I'll trade you a litre of Coke for it.'

I fished in my pocket, brought out the clay cow and handed it to her. She took out a blob of Prestick, put a piece under each foot and stuck it firmly on top of the till.

I stared at it. I couldn't believe I'd just made my first trade. It wasn't what I'd expected but a litre of Coke was certainly worth more than a lump of river clay.

I took the Coke out of the fridge, said, 'Thank you Mrs Viljoen!' and left the shop.

As soon as I got outside I punched the air with my fist and ran as fast as I could to Paki's house.

Chapter Seven

Paki lives at number 557 in a block house that is identical to ours. Except it has a white van parked outside on bricks and no peach tree.

'Hi Mrs Sebetso,' I called to Paki's mother.

Mrs Sebetso had a part-time job working the petrol pump at the garage. She was still wearing her pump attendant overalls and she was tinkering under the bonnet of the van. She used to spend all her spare time working on this white van. Every time someone asked she said, 'Nearly ready, nearly there.' She'd been saying that for two years now.

'Is Paki here?'

Mrs Sebetso waved at me and nodded at the house. Paki stuck his head out of a window.

'I got a Coke!' I said, and lifted it in the air.

'Good, but you have really messed up my cellphone – I've got two pieces here that don't seem to fit in anywhere.'

I went inside and found him sitting on his mother's bed fiddling with the cellphone. We took it apart again and as we fitted the pieces back together I told him the story.

'I'd better make you a new poster then,' he said. 'We should put it up next to the old one so that people can see how things are getting on.'

'Good idea,' I said, 'it'll be like a website.'

We went back to my house to make another poster, with the litre of Coke getting warmer and warmer in my hand.

When we got to my house we found my father eating lunch. He'd come home early because it was a Saturday. My grandmother was awake and taking the dry washing off the fence.

'What have you got there?' asked my father looking at the Coke in my hand.

'I got it from Mrs Viljoen at the café,' I replied, and told him the whole story.

My father was silent for a long time as he chewed his food. 'That's a good idea,' he said at last. 'You know the saying: "Shoot for the moon. Even if you miss it you will land among the stars." Let me see that story in the magazine.'

I showed him the magazine story and he read it aloud so that my grandmother could hear it as well.

'I don't understand this Internet thing,' said my grandmother. 'How did he get the paper clip into the Internet in the first place?'

I left Paki to explain how the Internet works while I went inside to get another piece of paper and the ballpoint pen.

To be honest I don't know much about the Internet, but we do have one computer at school that was donated by some overseas people. The school had to build a strong-room so that it doesn't get stolen. Once we each got a turn to use it and look up things using something called Google. I looked up the Kaizer Chiefs website but then the teacher kicked me off and told me it was someone else's turn.

My father was holding my Coke in his hand and smiling to himself.

'This is good,' he said. 'What you have here is something called a liquid asset. But it would be worth a lot more if it were cold. Can't you ask Mrs Viljoen if you can keep it in the fridge until you trade it?'

I didn't know what a liquid asset was, but I liked the idea of keeping the coke in the fridge.

'Come,' said Paki, 'we've got another poster to put up.'

Chapter Eight

Mrs Viljoen looked a bit uncertain when I asked her if I could have fridge space for the Coke. I showed her the magazine story so she could read about Kyle MacDonald for herself. There is something magical about that story because after she'd read it, she looked at me again over the top of her glasses and said I could put the Coke in her fridge.

'Hang on,' said Paki. 'You realise that this café is going to close at 5 o'clock this afternoon and it won't be open tomorrow because it's Sunday. So you won't be able to trade until Monday.'

I hadn't thought of that. 'I know. We'll go down to the soccer field this afternoon. The match being played there starts at 4 o'clock. We'll try and make a trade quickly before 5 o'clock. One of us can run up and get the Coke if we need to.'

'Good idea,' said Paki. 'There'll be lots of thirsty soccer players at the field.'

But we put up the poster and sat underneath

it in case anyone made us an offer we couldn't refuse before 4 o'clock.

No one did, but I didn't feel as foolish sitting there as I had that morning. The gang of guys outside the bottle store came over to look as we put up the poster. I noticed they didn't laugh at us quite so much as they had before.

There was not much life in the village that afternoon. About three cars passed on their way to Kokstad but no one stopped at the café.

Auntie Shirley from the library came to buy a packet of Marie biscuits and a candle.

'Ah, the famous clay cow boys,' she said when she saw us.

'I didn't know we were famous,' said Paki.

'Well maybe not *famous*,' said Auntie Shirley. 'But I have had two people in my library today telling me about your scheme. And I said to Meneer Venter when he told me, I said, "Meneer Venter, at last someone in this godforsaken town is trying to *do* something, instead of moaning." That's what I said to him.'

She tried to pat me on the head like the farmer's wife had done earlier, but I ducked when she put out her hand. I'm a fast learner.

'Come on,' said Paki, 'it's nearly 4 o'clock.'

Chapter Nine

There was the usual group of people gathered to watch the soccer match: a bunch of girls and all the younger boys of Cedarville. There was only soccer for the older boys. You had to be 15 and older to play. Mr Ndontso said that the younger boys caused too much trouble and didn't listen, so he refused to coach us.

Instead, we caused other kinds of trouble. Behind the soccer field was the old cheese factory where my father had worked before it closed down. Someone had cut a hole in the fence and we used to go there to break windows and find stuff to steal like door handles, old taps, that kind of thing. When there was nothing left to steal we just broke things. Sometimes we chased the sheep that kept the grass short around the factory.

The factory belongs to Mr Retief who also runs the Farmer's Co-op next door. He has a bad temper. Once he caught some of us in the old cold storage room. He said that if he ever caught us there again he would shut us in there for the whole weekend. So I hadn't been back.

The soccer players were at the far end of the field doing warm-up exercises.

The team from Kwabashe hadn't arrived yet. The Kwabashe players wear farm boots or play barefoot but they are as tough as anything and they play very dirty.

We had brought our poster and we stuck it up on a fence pole and waited.

A group of girls came over to us first. There were three of them walking in their high-heeled shoes with their arms linked so they didn't fall over in the lumpy grass.

Paki nudged me and spoke out of the corner of his mouth as they came closer. 'It's Nonhle and her friends.'

Nonhle is a grade above us at school and she is the most beautiful girl in Cedarville. I can hardly look at her – it's like looking at the sun. She is also my teacher's daughter.

Paki stared up at the sky as if he were searching for something. I picked at the grass. My heart was hammering.

'So what's the story about the Coke?' asked Nonhle. 'Are you selling it?'

I nudged Paki to do the talking. He nudged me back and carried on searching the sky.

'No . . . I am wanting to trade . . . um, that is, swap stuff . . . you see there's this guy in Canada, actually in a magazine, and he did this thing with a red paper clip on the Internet. He traded it for stuff and each time he traded he made sure it was for something with a higher value and then he . . . um . . . he got a house,' I gabbled.

'What?' asked Nonhle.

The other girls began to giggle.

Luckily Paki came to my rescue. 'He just wants to trade the Coke for something. Anything. He doesn't want money for it.'

I don't know if that made any more sense to them than my explanation but Nonhle nodded and walked off with her gang of friends.

Paki and I stared after them.

'Close your mouth,' said Paki. 'You look even more stupid with your mouth hanging open like that.'

I snapped my mouth shut and boxed him hard on the shoulder. We rolled around in the grass trying to hit each other.

'So which one of you has got this Coke I keep hearing about?' someone asked, towering over us.

We sat upright quickly.

It was Chipo, the goalie from the Cedarville soccer team. He was rubbing his leg.

'Um . . . that's me!' I said. 'Have you got something you want to trade?'

'Well I might have,' replied Chipo. 'I just need to go and check with the coach. Is the Coke cold?'

'Yes,' I replied. 'But you'll have to hurry because we have to fetch it from the fridge before 5 o'clock. It's at the café.'

Chipo limped off to find Mr Ndontso.

'It looks as if the Kwabashe team isn't going to arrive,' said Paki. 'Typical. Oh well, they'll just have to concede the match.'

Chipo and Mr Ndontso walked towards us. They dropped to their haunches to talk to us.

'We want to make a deal with you two,' said Mr Ndontso.

Chapter Ten

It was a complicated trade. I think Mr Ndontso had only agreed to it because the Cedarville team was at the top of the league and now that Kwabashe hadn't arrived for the match their position was even more secure.

It turned out that Chipo had a hamstring injury and needed to rest for about a week. As a trade for the bottle of Coke, Mr Ndontso agreed to let a younger player play in Chipo's place in next week's game against the Kokstad under-15Bs. He was hoping to find some new talent for the team and he needed a goalie reserve.

Chipo offered to share the Coke with Mr Ndontso, but he said that Chipo could keep the Coke – as long as he got a reasonable goalie.

'We'll give you a few minutes to talk about it, but I want to get home now, so don't take too long.'

Paki and I looked at his watch. We had 20 minutes before the café closed for the weekend.

'If we don't make a trade now, we won't be able to do anything until Monday afternoon,' said Paki.

'Yes, but we're not actually trading for anything proper.'

'What do you mean?'

'Well a place in the soccer team isn't really a . . . thing, is it?'

'No, but it might lead to a . . . thing.'

'OK, let's do it,' I said.

I sprinted to the café and got there just as Mrs Viljoen was about to lock up. When I arrived back at the soccer field I saw that almost everyone was still there.

I handed Chipo his Coke.

He nodded his thanks, unscrewed the lid and took a big, long drink. A few of the girls gave a cheer and clapped as he wiped his mouth with the back of his hand.

Some of the little boys jumped up at him begging for a sip, but he swatted them away with his free hand.

'Come Nonhle,' he said, 'I'll share it with you.'

The rest of the soccer team whooped and hit Chipo on the back.

But Nonhle just laughed and shook her head.

On the way home from soccer we had 20 offers for the place in the soccer team. Every boy under the age of 14 wanted a chance to play goalie in the next match. Some of them took off their dirty T-shirts as they walked and tried to give them to me.

'We will only consider serious offers,' shouted Paki above the noise. 'We'll be outside the café tomorrow morning. You can bring your offers there.'

'And don't bother bringing any dirty T-shirts!' I added loudly.

Chapter Eleven

The next morning I had to go to church with my grandmother. I had to walk her home afterwards, too, and she complained when I walked too fast. I tried to walk slowly but I was longing to get to the café.

After I'd left her at home I raced to the café and found Paki already there. He was surrounded by a crowd of children, some girls and most of the soccer team.

'We've come to do quality control,' explained Chipo. 'We want to make sure we get a good soccer player and not any old rubbish.'

'So that means *you*, *you*, *you* and *you* might as well go home,' said Sizwe, the captain of the team. He pointed at Jude, Mawili and two other, much younger boys. Jude and Mawili are absolutely hopeless at soccer and the other two both looked about five years old.

Everyone crowded around shoving things

at me: a bar of used soap with deep cracks in it, an old blanket, a bucket without a handle, a homemade catapult. They were all depressing options and definitely a step backwards from the place in the soccer team.

'Put everything against the wall,' said Paki. 'Boi will make his choice in his own time.'

Everyone rushed to put their stuff against the café wall. I noticed Paki had made another poster on a piece of cardboard to advertise the soccer position.

'Fulfil your dreams!' read the poster: 'A once-in-a-lifetime opportunity to play goalie for the Cedarville soccer team. To be traded for anything of value.' Paki had drawn a good picture of a soccer player in goalie gloves diving for the ball.

Suddenly there was the sound of a deep base beat, *DOEM chukka DOEM chukka*, and the roar of an engine. Mr Qokela, the taxi driver, pulled up outside the café. He left the engine running and the music blaring and walked up to where we stood.

'Where's Boipelo?' he asked.

Paki gave me a shove forward.

'I'm here.'

'I want to do a trade with you,' said Mr Qokela. 'I understand you are offering someone a chance to play goalie in the soccer team next Saturday.'

'Um . . . yes,' I said trying to look all businesslike.

Chapter Twelve

Mr Qokela made us a good offer, the best deal we had received so far. If we gave his son Aviwe a chance to play in the soccer match, he would give us a week's free transport in his taxi to Kokstad and back.

Paki and I talked it over quietly between us. It seemed like a good deal but there was a catch – Aviwe was slightly disabled. He had one leg that was much thinner than the other and a funny foot. He walked with a serious limp. He was always at the soccer practices and matches and he played goalie for us when we played soccer at school in the playground; he couldn't move fast but he had a good eye for the ball.

'It's a good deal, said Paki. 'A week's free transport is worth about . . .' he paused to do the sums.

'One hundred rand,' I said quickly. 'But what do you think Mr Ndontso is going to say when he finds out that Aviwe is going to be his goalie?'

'Nothing. Aviwe's not so bad you know, and they knew they were taking a bit of a risk anyway when they made the trade. Think of it this way: you'll be giving a guy a chance to play in the soccer team in a proper match. He'll probably never get that chance again.'

'Yes but . . .'

'Yes but nothing,' insisted Paki. 'It's either a hundred rand's worth of transport or half a bar of used soap. But you decide. You moron.' He kicked an empty cooldrink tin.

I went back to Mr Qokela and told him that I would have to check with Mr Ndontso before I made the trade.

'Well you know where to find me,' said Mr Qokela and drove off in his taxi.

Paki and I ran to the Full Gospel Church to find Mr Ndontso. Luckily he was still there when we arrived out of breath and panting.

We told him about the offer we'd had from Mr Qokela. And about Aviwe.

'He's actually got a good eye for the ball,' said Paki.

Mr Ndontso was silent for a while.

'Right,' he said eventually, 'you make sure Aviwe gets lots of practice before the game on Saturday – and I'll let him play. You never know . . . sometimes you find talent in the most unlikely places.'

Chapter Thirteen

The grown ups of Cedarville looking for transport were even worse than the young boys wanting a place in the soccer team. I was still asleep when the first offer came banging on our door, waking us all at 5 o'clock in the morning. It was Jimmy Claasens who lives on the other side of town.

'Yes, what is it?' grumbled my father when he flung open the door.

'I hear you're offering a week's free transport through to Kokstad and back.'

'Well, it's not exactly free,' said my father. 'You have to give my son something in return.'

'Have you got something to trade?' I asked him.

'Well I might and I might not,' said Jimmy looking shifty.

My father and I stared at him. Jimmy looked left and right and then quickly put his hand into his pocket and pulled out a big, gold watch.

I whistled.

'Thank you Jimmy. We are not interested,' said my father suddenly. He pulled me into the house and closed the door.

'What are you doing Dad?' I asked him, absolutely amazed.

'Where do you think someone like Jimmy Claasens got a gold watch from?' asked my father. He has a habit of asking me questions that he clearly knows the answer to.

'He stole it of course. And do you know why he wants the free transport through to Kokstad? He drinks so much and makes so much trouble that he's not allowed in the Cedarville bottle store any more. He wants to go through to Kokstad to drink.'

'Oh,' I said.

There was another offer before I even got to school: Mrs Eugenia Vuba, who lives a few houses away, came and knocked at the door soon after Jimmy Claasens had left. She was offering a matching duvet and pillow set still in its plastic bag. But my father closed the door on her as well. Apparently she has a boyfriend – in

Kokstad – that Mr Vuba doesn't know about. My father said it would cause trouble between them.

At school all the teachers had heard about the deal, too. One of them, whose name I won't mention, told me that if I gave him the transport, he'd make sure that I passed my Life Orientation test. I was quite tempted to take the offer but I knew it would leave me with nothing to trade after that. So I said 'no thanks' as politely as I could.

'What's going on with all of these grown ups?' I complained to Paki at break time. 'They all seem to be so . . . complicated.'

So when I got home from school and found Dana from the café waiting for me on the doorstep with a rusty, old wheelbarrow, I knew I would trade with her, whatever her story. I wanted to be rid of the free transport. It was making me uncomfortable.

It turned out that the reason Dana had not appeared for work on Saturday was because her little daughter Myra had been very sick. She had taken her to Kokstad to the hospital.

'She has to stay there for the whole week until she is better,' Dana told me. 'But she cries and cries if I am not with her. Mrs Viljoen has given me leave for a week to go and be with her. I really need this free transport, but all I can offer in exchange is this old wheelbarrow.'

'It's fine,' I said. 'We have a deal.'

I didn't think I had to check with Paki. I really thought I had made the right decision.

Chapter Fourteen

Paki came round later that afternoon. We were going to go together to give Aviwe some practice in the goals.

But he was not pleased with the deal I'd made.

'How could you do that without checking with me?' he asked. 'I had already offered it to Nelisiwe, and she was going to give us a free hair braiding and a hair treatment in exchange. It's worth more than this pile of old junk.' He kicked the wheelbarrow and it fell over.

'But it's not yours to offer!' I said. 'This is my idea. You can't do deals like that without me.'

Even as I said it, I felt bad because I knew that Paki had worked as hard as I had on this plan. Things were starting to feel complicated and difficult.

Paki took the soccer ball and left the house, slamming the door behind him.

I got out a piece of paper and the ballpoint pen and made a poster for the wheelbarrow. It didn't look nearly as good as Paki's posters.

When I arrived at the café to put it up I saw a small crowd of people had collected on the grass.

'What's going on?' I asked Prince.

'Someone from the *Kokstad Advertiser* has been taking photographs of the wall with your posters. There's a lady inside the café talking to Mrs Viljoen right now.'

'What for? What are they talking about?' I asked.

'I think she wants to write a story about you for the *Kokstad Advertiser*.'

'How did she find out about it?'

'I don't know. People talk I guess.'

I put up the new poster. A groan went up from the crowd when they saw that I had already traded the free transport. Some people had brought stuff they had hoped to trade. Everyone crowded round to look at the poster of the badly drawn wheelbarrow. They didn't seem as interested in it as they had been in the free transport.

I wished that Paki was there with me. I missed him, especially if I was going to have to answer questions from some lady from the *Kokstad Advertiser*. I felt a bit panicky. Would I have to talk to her in front of all these people?

I saw Nonhle in the crowd and she smiled at me. I don't know if that made me feel better or worse. I might make a fool of myself in front of her! I sat down under the posters with my head on my knees.

'Are you Boipelo?' asked a voice.

I looked up to see a lady standing against the sun. 'I'm from the *Kokstad Advertiser* and I want to ask you some questions about your clay cow idea. I want a photo of you in front of your posters. Then let's go somewhere private to talk.'

I stood up and a photographer started snapping pictures.

'Smile!' he said. 'Say cheese.'

But I didn't feel like smiling so I didn't.

The closest quiet place for us to talk was the library so I took her there. Most of the children followed behind us in a line, but when we got to the library Auntie Shirley shut the door and refused to let them in. I was very relieved. Some of them peeped in at the windows.

I told the lady about how I had got my idea and all about Kyle MacDonald and the red paper clip. I told her about the clay cow and about how Paki had helped me make posters. I made sure that I told her about Paki. I told her how we had traded the Coke for the position in the soccer team. And how Mr Qokela had given us a week's worth of free transport so that Aviwe could play in the match on Saturday. Then I told her about Dana and Myra and how Dana had given me the wheelbarrow in exchange for the free transport.

'What are you hoping to get at the end of all this?' she asked.

'Like Kyle MacDonald, I want a house,' I said. 'We live in a house that is very small. It is hot in summer and freezing in winter. I want a new house for my family.'

As I talked I realised that my plan did not include Paki. It didn't feel right but I didn't know what to do about it.

Chapter Fifteen

When I got home that evening I found my father busy fiddling with the wheelbarrow. 'This is going to need a bit of work,' he said. He wobbled the wheel, which looked as if it was about to fall off. The bottom of the wheelbarrow was rusted. 'And we'll have to reinforce this,' he added, 'but at least the frame is solid.'

I nodded. I was feeling bad about Paki and wished that we could fix the wheelbarrow together with my father. But part of me was still cross with him for thinking he could make decisions without me. Maybe he would come to me and apologise.

But Paki didn't come. I saw him at school the next day and he just ignored me. 'Forget it,' I thought. 'I'll go ahead and fix the wheelbarrow without him.'

After school I went to the bus graveyard next to the post office. It's full of old buses that are used for scrap. Most of the seats and steering wheels have been taken, but it's still possible to find stuff you need.

I found a nice, thick piece of metal that used to be part of a door. I had a screwdriver in my pocket and I carefully prised off some red and yellow reflectors and a rear-view mirror. I even found an old number plate lying in a clump of grass.

When I got home my father had already fixed the wheel with a piece of strong wire. It rotated quite smoothly now. He helped me to hammer the piece of metal flat and nail it over the rusty patch with some tiny nails.

It took me a few more days to attach the reflectors, the rear-view mirror and the number plate. I also decorated the wheel with some strips of metal that I had cut from a couple of empty Coke cans.

When it was finished the wheelbarrow looked great. It looked strong and a bit crazy and fun. I longed to take it round to Paki's house to show him what I had done, but I didn't.

While I had been working on the wheelbarrow,

I hadn't been going to the café after school. A few people had come to watch me work in the yard, but I had the feeling that people weren't as interested in the wheelbarrow as they had been in the free transport. Maybe Paki had been right and I had made a mistake with the trade.

I wheeled it round to the café on Thursday afternoon after school. I thought I would park it underneath the poster so that people could see what they would be getting.

When I got there I was in for a surprise. My posters, all five of them, were still up. And there were lots of other pieces of paper stuck to the wall, too.

'Lift wanted to Durban on Saturday. Speak to Kolotso at number 443 Mzingisi.'

'Kittens born at the Farmer's Co-op. Please speak to Pienkie if you can offer a good home.'

'A collection is being made for the funeral of Sizwe Mdlagathi – please give donations to Mrs Viljoen at the café.'

There were lots more notices.

There was the usual band of children and troublemakers hanging around; they were rolling

down the nearby grass bank and fooling about. But Mrs Viljoen didn't seem to mind them so much any more. I noticed that the guys from outside the bottle store had moved to this new venue as well. Quite a few of the farmers stopped to read the notices when they came to the café.

The younger children hopped inside the wheelbarrow and Mawili and Jude took turns pushing them up and down the pavement in front of the café.

I felt happier than I had in days, especially when I saw Nonhle. She took control of the children and made them stand in line for their turns.

But my heart sank when I saw Luvo walk over and start talking to her. What could he want to say to her? They seemed deep in conversation.

Then Luvo came up to me.

'I want that wheelbarrow,' he said.

'What can you trade?' I asked him.

'I've got a bag of this,' he replied, and pulled out a big bank bag stuffed with dagga from his pocket.

'It's good stuff,' he said, 'it's pure Durban Poison.'

Chapter Sixteen

A bag of dagga like that is potentially worth a lot of money. I knew plenty of people who would be very interested in it. But then how would I advertise it? I couldn't very well make a poster telling the whole world I had a bank bag stuffed full of dagga. I might even get knifed for it.

'Sorry,' I said reluctantly, 'no deal.'

Luvo was annoyed. 'I can use that wheelbarrow to earn some money,' he said. 'I really want it!'

I think Nonhle must have given him the idea of getting the wheelbarrow. He planned to wait with it near the taxi rank and help people to transport their shopping home when they arrived from Kokstad. Lots of people buy in bulk from the wholesalers there. Often they have to leave stuff on the pavement at the taxi rank while they take a load home. Then thieves steal the bags they have left behind. The wheelbarrow could be really useful.

'Can't you find something else to trade?' I asked him.

'I don't know,' he muttered miserably and walked off.

Nonhle went over to talk to him again. She must have given him an idea because I saw him walk purposefully down the street as if he had another plan.

While he was gone Mr Retief from the Farmer's Co-op arrived in his bakkie. He went into the café and came out carrying a magazine and a bottle of milk. Then he came and read the posters on the wall. Everyone behaved a bit more quietly when he was around; we were all scared of him.

'Is this it?' he asked, pointing at the crazy wheelbarrow. It was piled with children who were all looking at him with huge eyes.

'Yes Mr Retief,' I said.

'I'll trade you a 50 kilogram bag of mealie meal for it,' said Mr Retief. 'I could use that wheelbarrow in my stacking shed.'

A big bag of mealie meal is worth about R160. It would be a good deal.

But then I caught Nonhle's eye. She shook her head slightly. I knew that she wanted Luvo to get the wheelbarrow. And no way was I going to disappoint her.

'I'm sorry Mr Retief,' I said, 'I have already given it to someone else.'

Mr Retief slapped his leg and turned away impatiently. He got into his bakkie and drove away with an angry roar of the engine.

'You made the right decision,' said Nonhle when he was gone. 'Luvo will be back soon with something to trade. You'll see.'

She was right. Luvo did come back. He was holding a live chicken under his arm. A live chicken is only worth about R25. Any idiot could tell that was not a good deal. But if you added the fact that I had done something that pleased Nonhle to the cost of the live chicken . . . well, then the deal was brilliant. It was probably the best deal I had made so far. Or so I thought at the time.

Chapter Seventeen

I tucked the chicken tightly under my arm and walked home. I imagined what Paki would say when he heard about the deal I had passed up for this scrawny hen. I hoped that he would be waiting for me when I got home and that we'd able to laugh about it together.

But he wasn't there.

I tied the chicken's legs together and left it under the peach tree.

'Have you seen Paki?' I asked my grandmother.

'You know I can't see much,' she snapped at me.

I went to get the ballpoint pen and tried to make another poster. But I'm really bad at drawing – especially hens. I was on my third attempt when my father came home.

He leaned his spade and traffic cones against the wall of the house with a sigh and sat on the step to take off his muddy boots. I told him I'd traded Luvo the wheelbarrow for the chicken.

'It's not much of a chicken,' he said when he saw the hen lying blinking in the dust. I didn't tell him about Mr Retief's offer of the bag of mealie meal and I didn't tell him about Nonhle and how I'd tried to win her favour. There are some things you just can't talk about.

'Maybe you need to think about adding some value to this chicken,' suggested my father.

'What do you mean?' I asked.

'You know, when I worked at the cheese factory we had ways of adding value to the cheese so we could get more money for it. For example, if you slice cheese you can charge more money for it than if you sell the same quantity of cheese as a block. Or you can sell the cheese already grated. Or turn it into cheese sauce. That's called adding value.'

'OK, so if I kill the chicken and pluck it, that's adding value.' I paused to think about how this would work. 'Perhaps I could even offer to cook it! Kyle MacDonald traded his Coleman stove with the offer of a cooked meal.'

'Well that might work if you knew how to cook,' laughed my father.

'It can't be that hard,' I remember thinking.

Before I went to bed I made a new poster. It was easier to draw a pot with bits of chicken sticking out than to draw a real chicken.

That night I had terrible dreams: I dreamed that I had moved into Mrs Jackson's house and that Paki was knocking at the door and shouting at me to let him in. When I went to open the door I found the whole of Cedarville there trying to give me stuff to trade. Jimmy Claasens was trying to steal a wheelbarrow and Mrs Viljoen was hitting him over the head with an empty Coke bottle. The photographer from the *Kokstad Advertiser* kept shouting at me to 'SAY CHEESE!' and my father was shouting at me, 'NO! DON'T SAY IT! SLICE IT! SLICE IT OR TURN IT INTO CHEESE SAUCE!'

I woke up feeling terrible. And it only got worse when I arrived at school.

Chapter Eighteen

'Have you seen this Boipelo?' asked Mrs Jafta. She showed me the story that had appeared in the Friday edition of the *Kokstad Advertiser*. There was a photo of me scowling in front of the Cedarville café and the headline read: 'Cedarville Boy Trades Clay Cow for a Better Future'.

The article that followed described how I had got the idea from Kyle MacDonald and his red paper clip. And then it went into detail about all the trades I had made. The story made it seem like I was some kind of saint: giving a crippled boy a chance to play in a soccer team, enabling a mother to visit her sick child in hospital, and so on.

I scanned the article quickly for any mention of Paki.

Nothing. Not one word.

I felt sick reading it. It sounded as if I had told the journalist all about how wonderful I was and had forgotten to tell her about Paki. But I had told her that Paki had drawn all the posters and how we had done everything together. Now, however, I knew that whatever I told Paki, he wouldn't believe me.

I found Paki at break time. He, Prince and Mawili were giving Aviwe goalie practice against the fence with a deflated soccer ball. Aviwe was doing quite well – diving all over the place and making some good saves.

'Paki, I need to talk to you,' I said. 'That story in the newspaper . . .'

'Is all about just how wonderful you are,' Paki interrupted.

'No! The lady didn't write what I told her,' I pleaded. 'I told her about you and everything you have done.'

'Well maybe you just didn't tell her loudly enough,' said Paki and gave the soft soccer ball a mighty kick that sent it flying over the fence.

He disappeared to fetch it and left me standing on my own in the playground.

Chapter Nineteen

Mrs Jafta was busy locking up the classroom to go home when she stopped me. Nonhle was with her; they always walked home together after school.

'What are you going to do with that chicken Boi?' she wanted to know.

I told her what my father had suggested about adding value. 'I'm thinking I'll offer to cook it for the person who wants to trade with me.'

'That's an interesting idea.' She paused and then said, 'Mr Zulu from the Department of Education is coming to do a workshop for the teachers on Saturday. He will be staying at my house tonight. If I provided you with the ingredients would you be able to cook the chicken for our dinner?'

'Yes!' I said without even thinking. If I cooked the chicken I could spend the whole evening at Nonhle's house. Of course I would do it. I didn't even really care what she wanted to trade.

'I've got a box-set of Chuck Norris DVDs that I'm happy to trade for the cooked chicken,' said Mrs Jafta. 'I think there are four DVDs in the box. Is that OK with you?'

Chuck Norris! A box-set!

'Yes of course! Thank you Mrs Jafta!' I said. 'What time shall I come round?'

She looked at her watch. 'It's 2 o'clock now . . . let's say 4 o'clock. That should give you plenty of time to cook the chicken for supper.'

On my way home I stopped at the café. There were the usual people hanging around and I told them that Mrs Jafta had offered to trade me the cooked chicken for her set of Chuck Norris DVDs.

That caused some excitement and a few of the children raced home to tell their parents.

I don't like killing chickens, but I only had an hour before I went to Mrs Jafta's house, and I couldn't put it off any longer. I hate the way a chicken carries on flapping about when its head is off. But I did it quickly and took it to my grandmother for plucking. She does a good job and can remove even the tiniest feathers. I put the wet chicken in a packet.

On the way to Mrs Jafta's house a little girl ran up to me. 'There's a man in a big, black Land Rover with a Durban registration number who was looking for you,' she said. 'I told him to go to your house.'

I didn't think much about it at the time. I was so busy dreaming about Nonhle and the evening I would be spending at her house. I passed the soccer field. Mr Qokela and Aviwe were practising for the big match tomorrow and I waved at them. It made me happy to see them.

Chapter Twenty

'I've got some rice, a pumpkin and cooking oil,' said Mrs Jafta, pointing to a pile of groceries on the kitchen counter. 'And here are a few onions, Aromat and some carrots.'

She showed me where the knife and pots were kept under the counter. 'And you'll need to use these pliers to turn the stove on because the knob has broken. I'll leave you to get on with it. I'm going to pick up Mr Zulu from the taxi rank. He's coming all the way from Mthatha so he'll probably be tired. Oh and here's an apron – you don't want chicken fat on your clothes.'

Mrs Jafta left. I could see Nonhle outside in the garden. She was having her hair braided by her friend Reanetse and they were talking and laughing together. I felt a bit shy but I went outside to talk to them.

'Hi!' called Nonhle when she saw me. 'How are you going to cook the chicken? I love chicken, it's my favourite.'

'Oh I'll probably just make a stew,' I said casually as if I knew what I was doing.

'I like boys who can cook,' said Reanetse. 'I'm going to make sure I marry a good cook!'

It was about then that I really started to panic. I'd never made a chicken stew in my life. I'd seen my grandmother cook chicken and rice and I wished I'd paid more attention. I had a vague idea that she chopped the vegetables first.

So I chopped the carrots and onions and poured a lot of the Aromat and cooking oil over them. Then I chopped up the chicken with the blunt knife. Next I chopped the pumpkin. I was sweating by the time I had finished.

The kitchen looked very messy. There were peels and onion skins everywhere.

I put the chicken in a pot and turned on the stove with the pliers as I'd been told.

I left the chicken to cook and turned my attention to the rice. On the way from the sink to the stove the rice slopped out of the pot all over the floor. I scooped it up with my hands and put it back in the pot.

The next half hour was the most stressful time of my life.

The rice grew like a monster and spilled over the sides of the small pot. It kept burning at the bottom. And the chicken was a disaster. Much of it was burnt before I thought of adding water and then I added too much. The burnt chunks bobbed about in the water like a strange soup. In desperation I threw in the vegetables just as Mrs Jafta came in the door with Mr Zulu from the Department of Education.

'It smells . . .' Mrs Jafta paused. I knew she would have liked to have said, 'It smells delicious!' but all she said was, 'It smells . . .'

'This is the special boy I was telling you all about Mr Zulu – Boipelo Xaba. He is cooking our supper tonight.'

'Ah,' said Mr Zulu, 'I've been hearing wonderful things about you, Boipelo. It's fantastic when learners take initiative like you have done. Congratulations young man.' He held out his hand for me to shake.

I wiped my greasy hands on the apron and shook his hand.

When he'd gone to wash his hands for supper, Mrs Jafta came back into the kitchen. She looked very upset. 'What's going on in here Boi?' She lifted the lids of the pots and looked anxiously inside.

'I'm sorry Mrs Jafta. This cooking business is more complicated than I thought.'

'We can't eat this!' said Mrs Jafta in an anxious whisper. 'This just isn't good enough. I could never feed him this! Quickly clean up. I'll have to make some eggs and tea instead.' She looked sternly across at me, 'I certainly can't give you that box-set of DVDs. I'm afraid the deal is off.'

I cleaned up the kitchen as quickly as I could before Nonhle came inside, apologised to Mrs Jafta again and quietly left the house.

Chapter Twenty-one

I was grateful for the darkness. As I ran, tears streamed down my face as I thought of everything I had lost: I had nothing to trade any more, I had lost Paki, and now Nonhle would think I was the greatest idiot in the world.

When I got home my father was sitting under the peach tree. I hoped he wouldn't see my tears.

'There was a man here earlier looking for you,' he said. 'He said he was from the *Sunday Times*. He wants to talk to you.'

'There's nothing to tell,' I said. 'I tried to cook the chicken for Mrs Jafta this evening and I ruined it. So I have nothing left to trade. It's all over.'

'Well I told him that you would be here at about 8 o'clock tomorrow morning,' said my father.

I sighed and went off to bed.

The next morning I woke early while it was

still dark and slipped quietly out of the house. I wanted to get away from everyone. I didn't want to have to explain how I had ruined the chicken. I didn't want to face Paki and I didn't want to see Nonhle.

Behind Cedarville is a big mountain that I had never been up before. It was hard work climbing it now; I could hardly see the big rocks and dongas in the moonlight. But soon the sky began to lighten in the east. The sun rose over the Bokkiesberg mountains and lit up the flats and the ribbon of river that runs east of the village.

Everything seemed very different from up there: the roads in the village looked straight and the buildings looked tidy and clean. I could see my house and Paki's house. I could even see his mother's white van parked in the yard. It looked like a toy van.

I sat thinking for a long time. At first I was boiling with feelings.

How will I ever make peace with Paki?

How could I have been so stupid as to think I could cook?

What does Nonhle think of me?

I have lost everything!

I picked up stones to hurl down the mountain. Some of them exploded when they hit bigger rocks. I threw more and more until my arm ached.

When I turned around to pick up more stones, I saw the moon still in the sky. What was that stupid thing my father had told me? 'Shoot for the moon. Even if you miss it you will land among the stars.' It should be, 'Shoot for the moon. When you miss it, you will land with your stupid face in the mud!'

I threw a stone at the moon and sat down with a sob.

When I looked up a long-tailed widow bird was hovering above the grass, showing off his beautiful tail. 'Look at me! Look at me!' he seemed to be insisting.

Some Egyptian geese flew over me, honking on their way to the river. I could hear the *whap whap* of their wings as they flew just above my head.

Slowly the lump of disappointment and regret in my chest began to melt away. I began to get ideas of what I needed to do: I needed to earn some money and buy another chicken. I needed to be able to carry on trading . . .

But first I needed to go and talk to Paki. I got up to go and suddenly my eye was caught by the flash of sunlight on a windscreen. It was a black Land Rover and it seemed to be heading for my house.

I ran down the mountain as fast as I could. When I got home there was a man under the peach tree talking to my grandmother.

'Sorry I'm late,' I gasped. 'I will talk to you but you have to promise me something . . .'

Chapter Twenty-two

It was about 10 o'clock when I eventually got to the café. There was a big crowd of people all wanting to know about the DVDs. I had to tell them that the deal was off but that soon I would have another chicken to trade.

Mr Retief had put up a notice on the wall asking for a sweeper in his packing shed. He was offering to pay R20 a day. I would only be able to work after school and he'd probably say 'no', especially after I'd refused his offer of the mealie meal trade. But I ripped the notice off the wall and ran to the Farmer's Co-op. I had to try.

'Oh it's you,' said Mr Retief when he saw me standing in his office clutching the notice. 'I thought you were busy cooking chickens and what-have-you. What do you want this job for?'

I told him the story of the burnt chicken and how I wanted to get back into trading by buying another chicken.

He hesitated and then agreed to give me the job. It was just a temporary position. Rats had made holes in the bags in the packing shed and Mr Retief was busy poisoning them. He needed someone to clean up the mess they had made.

He gave me a big, heavy broom and showed me the packing shed. It was huge. I swept for hours until I got blisters.

At about 5 o'clock Mr Retief came and gave me R15 because I hadn't done a full day's work. He said he would see me on Monday after school.

If I hurried I would still have time to get to the soccer match. I wanted to see Aviwe in action and I could hear the sound of the crowd and some vuvuzelas in the distance.

The quickest route was through the grounds of the cheese factory. So as soon as Mr Retief had left I wriggled through the hole in the fence. Three of the sheep escaped through the hole after me. I threw stones at them to make them go back but they trotted off down the road. The soccer match was almost over! I didn't have time to chase after them. I hoped no one had seen me and sprinted off towards the game.

The soccer match was nearly over by the time I got there. There was the biggest crowd, including lots of grown ups, I'd ever seen at a Cedarville match. Aviwe was doing really well. The score was 3–2 to the Kokstad under-15Bs but Cedarville had possession and looked as if they might score. Sizwe took a free kick but the Kokstad defence was strong and booted the ball right up the field. Aviwe steadied himself for another save . . . but then the whistle blew to signal the end of the match.

Cedarville had lost, but not badly, and Aviwe was the hero of the day. His team hoisted him up on their shoulders and ran with him around the field while everyone cheered and the vuvuzelas mooed like cows. I looked everywhere for Paki but couldn't find him in the crowd. I really needed to talk to him.

Chapter Twenty-three

On Sunday morning I woke up with a lump in my heart. I knew I had to talk to Paki today and the longer I delayed doing it, the heavier the lump became.

I was sitting on the step outside our house eating a bowl of phutu and milk when Siyabulela, one of the little boys who lives at the end of our street, came running down the road.

'It's Mr Retief!' he shouted as soon as he saw me. 'He's coming! He's coming to your house!'

I stopped eating and put down my bowl. Suddenly I felt sick. I was convinced Mr Retief had discovered the missing sheep and was coming... to do what? Beat me? Fire me from my job?

Mr Retief's bakkie roared up to our house. He got out and slammed the door. He had a rolled up newspaper under his arm. Maybe he was going to whack me with the rolled up newspaper.

'Where's your father Boipelo?' he asked gruffly.

'He's inside,' I squeaked, and scrambled off the step to go and call him. But my father was already there, wiping his hands on a towel.

'Mr Xaba, I need to talk to you,' said Mr Retief.

My father beckoned him into our house. They shut the door behind them and left me on the doorstep.

It was the longest five minutes of my life. I could only just make out the sound of their deep voices talking inside but I couldn't hear what they were saying. I had a deep feeling of dread.

Suddenly the door flew open and my father told me to come inside. I looked at his face to see if he was angry with me but I couldn't interpret his expression.

Mr Retief was sitting on my grandmother's bed.

There were a few moments of silence as they both looked at me. My heart was bouncing like a tennis ball.

My father cleared his throat and said, 'Boi, Mr Retief has come to make a trade with you.'

'But Mr Retief, I have nothing to trade. I told you yesterday that I'd lost the chicken. That's why I needed the job.'

'You do have something to trade,' said Mr Retief, 'something very valuable actually.' He spread the Sunday newspaper out on my grandmother's bed and turned to an inside page.

'Look here,' he said.

'Clay Cowboys Change Lives', read the headline. There were three photos: a close-up of me scowling that had been taken by the *Kokstad Advertiser*, one of Paki in his school uniform and a picture of Mrs Viljoen standing at her till with the clay cow stuck on top.

I read the story. It was about two boys from Cedarville, Boipelo and Paki, and how they had worked together to try to change their lives. Boipelo had the original idea and Paki had drawn the posters. They had done everything together and brought happiness to quite a few people in Cedarville. The story even described how Boipelo had burnt the chicken and was determined to earn money to buy another one and start trading again.

'I still don't understand Mr Retief. What can I trade? I have nothing left,' I said.

'Do you realise what this kind of publicity is worth?' asked Mr Retief. 'Today the whole country is going to read about the Clay Cowboys. People love reading stories like this when there is so much ugliness everywhere.'

He paused. 'When I read this story this morning I got an idea. I have been wanting to re-open the cheese factory and start making cheese again. But it seemed impossible: a small factory in a small town and no money for advertising . . . But now that the village of Cedarville is getting famous, all thanks to your strange trading business, maybe enough people will notice us. Maybe they will notice my cheese. But the cheese will sell even better if you let me use your name.'

'Boipelo cheese?'

'No man. I want to call it *Clay Cow Cheese*,' said Mr Retief. 'That's what I want to trade with you.'

'But what will you give me in return?' I asked, still confused by this offer.

'Well I can't really offer *you* much I'm afraid,' said Mr Retief. 'But I can offer your father a job helping me to get it all set up. I could do with his experience in cheese production.'

I felt a big grin spread over my face. 'OK,' I said. 'But I will have to go and speak to Paki about it. There are two of us clay cowboys.'

'Off you go then cowboy,' said my father as he and Mr Retief shook hands.

'Thank you,' said Mr Retief. 'I have a good feeling about this.'

I was half way out the door when I had a sudden idea.

'You don't think that maybe you are going to need a van to transport the cheese? I know of a white van that only needs a set of wheels that might do nicely.'

Mr Retief nodded. 'I'll think about it,' he said.

Chapter Twenty-four

And so that is the story of how I traded a clay cow for a cheese factory. It wasn't the dream house that I had started out thinking I wanted. But now that my father has a proper job we have been able to afford ceiling boards and electricity. Maybe one day we'll be able to build a small bedroom for me. In the meantime I'm still sleeping on the floor next to my grandmother.

In many ways the town of Cedarville is still the same. You'd have to have sharp eyes to see the changes, but they are there: the cheese factory has started small and only employs four people. One of those, of course, is my father and another is Paki's mother who drives a small, white van with 'Clay Cow Cheese' written on the side.

The other thing you might notice is that the Cedarville soccer team wears kit that says 'Clay Cow Cheese' on the back. Just ask for the 'cowboys' and you'll probably find Paki and I hanging out around the soccer field together. I'll be the boy holding hands with Nonhle, the prettiest girl in Cedarville.

I have a plan to write to Kyle MacDonald and ask him to come and visit Cedarville one day. If he comes by taxi Luvo will carry his suitcase for free in the strangest wheelbarrow he's ever seen. And we'll give him a big wheel of Clay Cow Cheese to take home. I think it would make him happy.